APR - - 2018

Buffy Sainte-Marie

Musician, Indigenous Icon, and Social Activist

Linda Barghoorn

Crabtree Publishing Company

www.crabtreebooks.com

Author: Linda Barghoorn

Series research and development: Reagan Miller

Editorial director: Kathy Middleton

Editor: Ellen Rodger

Proofreader: Wendy Scavuzzo

Photo researchers: Samara Parent

Designer and prepress technician: Samara Parent

Print coordinator: Katherine Berti

Photographs:
Alamy: © WENN Ltd: cover

AP Photo: © Dave Pickoff: page 9

The Canadian Press: © Justin Tang: pages 4-5, 25; © John Mahler / Toronto Star: page 14; © CP PHOTO: pages 20-21, 23; © Winnipeg Free Press-David Lipnowski: page 22; © Chris Young: page 27; © Sean Kilpatrick: page 28; © Adrian Wyld: page 29

Getty Images: © David Gahr: page 10; © Michael Ochs Archives: page 11; © Bettmann: page 12; © John Mahler / Toronto Star: page 14; © Andrew Putler / Redferns: page 15; © Fred W. McDarrah: pages 16-17; © Jim Russell / Toronto Star via Getty Images: page 18; © Terry Wyatt / Getty Images for Americana Music: page 19; © C Brandon / Redferns: page 24; © ABC Photo Archives: page 26

Public Domain: page 8

Wikimedia Commons: © Drpeterstockdale: title page; © Nationaal Archief: page 13; © Bamble kommune: page 30

All other images from Shutterstock

About the author: Linda Barghoorn has been sharing stories—hers and others—for years. She has interviewed rap musicians, TV news anchors, and most importantly, her dad. She is the author of several children's books and is working on a novel about her father's life.

Library and Archives Canada Cataloguing in Publication

Barghoorn, Linda, author
   Buffy Saint-Marie : musician, indigenous icon, and social activist / Linda Barghoorn.

(Remarkable lives revealed)
Includes index.
Issued in print and electronic formats.
ISBN 978-0-7787-4709-3 (hardcover).--
ISBN 978-0-7787-4715-4 (softcover).--
ISBN 978-1-4271-2077-9 (HTML)

   1. Sainte-Marie, Buffy--Juvenile literature. 2. Women singers--Canada--Biography--Juvenile literature. 3. Singers--Canada--Biography--Juvenile literature. 4. Cree women--Canada--Biography--Juvenile literature. I. Title. II. Series: Remarkable lives revealed

ML3930.S14B37 2018   j782.42164092   C2017-907728-7
                                                                           C2017-907729-5

Library of Congress Cataloging-in-Publication Data

Names: Barghoorn, Linda, author.
Title: Buffy Saint-Marie : musician, indigenous icon, and social activist / Linda Barghoorn.
Description: New York, New York : Crabtree Publishing, [2018] | Series: Remarkable lives revealed | Includes index.
Identifiers: LCCN 2017057537 (print) | LCCN 2017058607 (ebook) | ISBN 9781427120779 (Electronic HTML) | ISBN 9780778747093 (reinforced library binding : alk. paper) | ISBN 9780778747154 (pbk. : alk. paper)
Subjects: LCSH: Sainte-Marie, Buffy--Juvenile literature. | Women singers--Canada--Biography--Juvenile literature. | Singers--Canada--Biography--Juvenile literature. | Cree women--Canada--Biography--Juvenile literature.
Classification: LCC n-cn--- (ebook) | LCC ML3930.S14 B37 2018 (print) | DDC 782.42164092 [B] --dc23
LC record available at https://lccn.loc.gov/2017057537

Crabtree Publishing Company
www.crabtreebooks.com   1-800-387-7650

Printed in the U.S.A./032018/BG20180202

Published in Canada
Crabtree Publishing
616 Welland Ave.
St. Catharines, Ontario
L2M 5V6

Published inthe United States
Crabtree Publishing
PMB 59051
350 Fifth Ave., 59th Floor
New York, NY 10118

Published in theUnited Kingdom
Crabtree Publishing
Maritime House
Basin Road North, Hove
BN41 1WR

Published in Australia
Crabtree Publishing
3 Charles Street
Coburg North
VIC, 3058

Contents

Between Two Worlds

Our life stories are woven together by the challenges we face and the lessons we learn as we grow up. Other people's life stories can inspire us to learn more about the world in which we live. When they make extraordinary things happen, these people motivate us to explore our own potential to change the world.

What Is a Biography?

A biography is the story of a person's life. We read biographies to learn about another person's thoughts and experiences. Biographies can be based on many sources of information. Primary sources include a person's own words or pictures. Secondary sources come from friends, family, media, and research.

Buffy has performed her music professionally on stage for more than 50 years.

Buffy Sainte-Marie

Some people have remarkable stories of **activism**, creativity, or determination. As a singer and activist of Cree heritage, Buffy Sainte-Marie has spoken out about the challenges faced by **Indigenous** peoples. Her music has always reflected her strong beliefs about love, **spirituality**, and identity. Her passion, energy, and commitment have shaped a career that has lasted more than 50 years. As you read about Buffy, think about her roles as a musician, artist, activist, educator, and **humanitarian**.

Cree Heritage

The Cree are one of the largest Indigenous groups in North America. Their traditional territory stretches from parts of Quebec, Canada, to the Northwest Territories.

Indigenous Heritage

Buffy Sainte-Marie was born in 1941 on the Piapot Plains Cree First Nation **Reserve** in Saskatchewan, Canada. As a child, Buffy was adopted by Alfred and Winifred Sainte-Marie and grew up in Massachusetts. Although Winifred was of **Mi'kmaq** heritage, she taught Buffy very little about Indigenous culture. But she warned her not to believe everything that was written about Indigenous people in history books.

Adopted Out

For many years in the mid-1900s, Indigenous children in Canada were adopted out of their culture. This often meant they lost contact with their Indigenous heritage. Some children also suffered racism and abuse.

Buffy was born in the Qu'Appelle Valley in the province of Saskatchewan, Canada.

Love of Music

Buffy was often bullied because she was different. Her love of music gave her an escape. She banged on pots and pans, blew on blades of grass, and played with rubber bands to make different sounds. She even took apart her mother's vacuum cleaner and tried to create headphones by connecting its tubes to her broken record player.

"
As a little kid when I was three, I discovered a piano and I found out it made noise and I was fascinated…

—Buffy Sainte-Marie, *Vogue* magazine, 2015
"

Understanding Her Roots

As a young woman, Buffy visited the Piapot reserve, where she took part in a traditional **powwow** ceremony and was unofficially adopted by one of Chief Piapot's sons. Learning about her heritage allowed Buffy to discover her place in Indigenous culture. She would become a passionate spokesperson for Indigenous rights.

Chief Piapot

Born in 1816, Chief Piapot saw dramatic changes to his people's way of life. European settlers took over their land. The buffalo, a main source of food, were dwindling because of overhunting. Piapot was a respected leader who guided his people, worked out land treaties, and fought against the loss of Cree culture.

The Cree Nation

The Cree, or Nehiyawak, are a large group of Indigenous people. Many different bands, or groups, of Cree people have lived in North America for thousands of years. They believe that health and happiness are achieved by living in balance with nature. Art and music are important parts of Cree culture.

> " It's interesting that my family's named Piapot... an Assiniboine word that means "between two". Because this is real typical of me too: between two cultures, between two families, between two countries.
>
> —CBC Music, The Vault, 1994 "

? THINK ABOUT IT

Why does Buffy feel she lives "between two"?

Buffy married Sheldon Wolfchild in 1975. They had a son before their marriage ended.

Launching a Music Career

Buffy continued to develop her love of music. In high school, she was already writing songs and had learned to play guitar and piano. Later, as a student at university, she began to discover new cultures, ideas, and music by other singers. These would all influence her musical style and what she sang about. Buffy often played for friends, who encouraged her to perform publicly. So, she began playing in front of small audiences in Toronto and New York.

*Buffy plays for a **folk** festival audience in 1967.*

Pursuing a Love of Music

When Buffy was 21 years old, she graduated among the top 10 in her university class. She had always loved teaching and learning, but decided to take a break to pursue her love of music. She moved to New York City, where she found herself performing with other young musicians such as Joni Mitchell, Neil Young, and Leonard Cohen.

Soon she was touring the United States, Canada, and Europe. People praised her unique style and musical creativity. Buffy found her success surprising. She had never considered herself a talented singer.

Buffy taught herself to play piano and guitar, and her style influenced other musicians.

Her First Record Contract

A year later, Buffy had a recording contract and released her first album called *It's My Way!* She was named Best New Artist in 1964 and quickly became famous as a **folk** singer. Her songs explored many themes—from love and war to **human rights** and addiction. As she traveled, Buffy discovered that the challenges facing Indigenous people were similar everywhere. She was determined to use her music to help educate others about Indigenous people and issues.

> *The music business didn't know or care that I was an educator or a painter.*
>
> —*It's My Way*, CBC News, 2014

Imaginative and Curious

Imaginative and curious, Buffy enjoyed experimenting with sound and technique. Her vibrating singing style was influenced by listening to Indigenous powwow singing and music by French singer Edith Piaf. Buffy often used a mouth bow to create unique sounds. She was the first person to use Indigenous beats in rock music. She labeled her song "Starwalker" "powwow rock" music.

Drum Circle

The drum is the heartbeat of all powwow ceremonies and music.

? THINK ABOUT IT

What are some of the unique qualities of Buffy's music?

A mouth bow is a stringed instrument that looks like an archery bow.

Messages Through Music

Buffy writes about issues that are close to her heart. Her song "Now That the Buffalo's Gone" argued against governments taking Indigenous lands. In "Universal Soldier," she sang about everyone's responsibility for war. "My Country 'Tis of Thy People You're Dying" was about the **oppression** of Indigenous peoples. Buffy challenged her listeners to learn about issues and to correct the mistakes of the past. She shares a different version of North American history—one that is often ignored. It tells of the perspectives of Indigenous peoples.

Buffy has always used her voice and profile as an artist to promote issues close to her heart, including Indigenous rights and education.

Year After Year

Buffy is a very productive songwriter. Between 1964 and 1976, she released an album every year. Her songs are enjoyed by audiences and artists in many countries around the world. One of her biggest hits was a love song called, "Until It's Time for You to Go." It has been recorded in 16 languages by more than 200 different artists. Buffy had many powerful messages she wanted to share with the world.

> "I try to tell the story that's left out of the history books.
>
> —From the album *Little Wheel Spin and Spin*, 1966"

Inspiring the World

Buffy's songs inspire listeners with a deeper sense of their shared **humanity**. Through her music, she reminds everyone that we are all connected to each other and the planet we share. She is keenly aware of the power of words and music to help educate and create change.

> " Sometimes you can artfully say something in a three-minute song that it would take somebody else a 400-page book to write.
>
> —*Democracy Now!* special, 2009 "

Buffy sang at the 1963 March on Washington for Jobs and Freedom, a civil rights rally.

Outspoken and Unapologetic

Buffy's willingness to speak out almost immediately drew the attention of the American government. It didn't approve of her opinions about war and Indigenous rights. In the 1970s, she was **blacklisted** by the government, which claimed that her music encouraged improper public protests. She was warned to stop singing about such issues, but she continued without apology. Radio stations were ordered not to play her music. For several years, Buffy almost disappeared from public radio.

? THINK ABOUT IT

Why did the U.S. government blacklist Buffy Sainte-Marie's music?

Philanthropy and Activism

As an activist, Buffy Sainte-Marie has devoted much of her career to highlighting Indigenous issues including land rights, racism, and education. She is determined to erase the **stereotypes** of Indigenous people. Buffy educates people about the positive role of Indigenous people in modern society. She is committed to providing Indigenous youth with better opportunities for education. As an artist, she has fought to have Indigenous actors represented on television.

Helping kids is important to Buffy. She has developed curriculum and spoken widely about education.

Nihewan Foundation

Buffy's successful music career provided the money to support her **philanthropy** work. In 1969, she created the Nihewan Foundation. Its goals reflect her strong belief in the potential of Indigenous people through improved education. The word *Nihewan* comes from the Cree language. It means "talk Cree"—suggesting that Indigenous people should take pride in their culture and keep it alive.

> " The reality of the situation is that [Indigenous peoples are] not all dead and stuffed in some museum with the dinosaurs.
>
> — **Cradleboard.org website, 2002** "

Buffy accepts the Spirit of Americana Award from Jed Hilly of the Americana Music Association in 2015. Americana music is a mixture of folk, country, blues and other styles.

Helping Indigenous Youth

Many Indigenous youth educated on reserves face difficulty pursuing a college or university education. Through her foundation, Buffy created a fund that provides scholarships, or money, to help students get an education. The foundation prepares students for college or university, supports them as they leave home, and promotes their right to play a role in the global community.

Always willing to back up her beliefs, Buffy sings here at a benefit for the Piapot Reserve in 1975. The concert raised money to build a school.

Promoting Global Understanding

The Nihewan Foundation's Youth Council on Race gives Indigenous teenagers an opportunity to discuss racial and identity issues online with teens from other cultures. These discussions help them form a better understanding of one another, and find common solutions to problems. The foundation's Cradleboard Teaching Project provides Indigenous students with research materials about their culture. Buffy feels these materials help **empower** Indigenous youth with knowledge about their cultures.

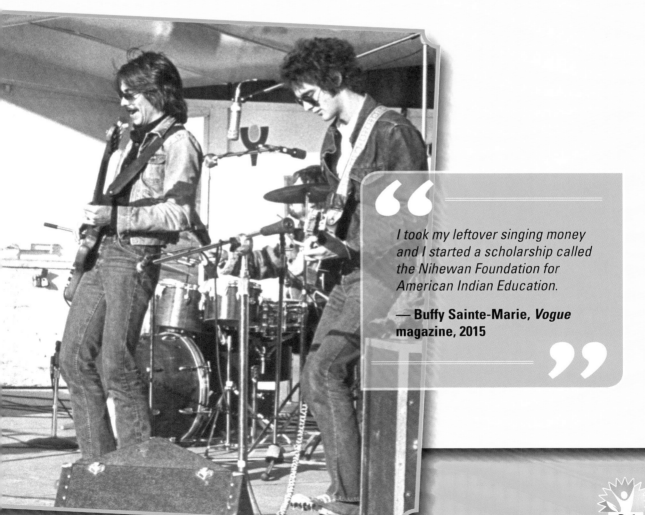

" I took my leftover singing money and I started a scholarship called the Nihewan Foundation for American Indian Education.

— **Buffy Sainte-Marie, *Vogue* magazine, 2015**

Film and TV Work

Buffy has also worked to raise awareness of Indigenous people through film. She appeared in the 1985 documentary, *Broken Rainbow*, about the forced relocation of Indigenous people in Arizona. It won an Academy Award for Best Documentary Feature that year. Buffy has written and performed music for numerous projects. She wrote the music for *Where the Spirit Lives*. This is a Canadian film about Indigenous children kidnapped and forced into **residential schools**. Buffy also wrote the theme music for *Spirit Bay*, the first all-Indigenous TV series in Canada.

Actor Gordon Toottoosis gives Buffy a Lifetime Achievement award at the Aboriginal People's Choice Awards in 2009.

Sesame Street Star

In 1976, Buffy put her music career aside to raise her newborn son, Dakota ('Cody') Starblanket Wolfchild. When the producers of *Sesame Street* asked her to appear on their television show, she agreed. She often brought Cody along. Buffy used the opportunity to teach children about Indigenous culture. During her five years on *Sesame Street,* she shared many songs and stories of Indigenous peoples. She also taught The Count how to count in the Cree language. Children in more than 70 countries watched and learned from her.

? THINK ABOUT IT

Why did Buffy create the Nihewan Foundation?

Buffy and her son Dakota Starblanket Wolfchild were regulars on Sesame Street in the 1970s.

A Lifelong Career

Buffy has always enjoyed experimenting with music and art. She was one of the first musicians to introduce technology into her music when she used a **synthesizer** to change instrumental and vocal sounds. Buffy merged technology, music, and art, and created a multimedia production called *Science: Through Native American Eyes*. Part of her Cradleboard teaching project, it helps students explore science, history, and culture, as seen through the eyes of Indigenous people.

A synthesizer is one tool that helps Buffy explore new sounds.

Yesterday and Today

Buffy's songs have been covered by hundreds of artists during her career. In the 1970s, The "King of Rock and Roll" Elvis Presley sang her love ballad "Until It's Time for You to Go." More than 40 years later, Kanye West sampled her music in his work. Buffy has also inspired and worked with many Indigenous artists and performers. The electronic music group A Tribe Called Red remixed her song, "Working for the Government." Buffy also worked with Inuit throat singer, Tanya Tagaq. They released a song about Indigenous Alaskan dogsledder, George Attla, called "You Got to Run."

Throat Singing

Throat singing is a form of Inuit music in which singers use rhythmic vocal or breathing patterns to create music.

Buffy has inspired new generations of Indigenous artists, including Tanya Tagaq and A Tribe Called Red.

More Music

In 1982, Buffy co-wrote a song, "Up Where We Belong." It would be her biggest hit, winning many awards, including an Academy Award and a Grammy. Buffy was the first Indigenous person ever to win an Academy Award. After a long break, she returned to making records in 1993, and has continued ever since. In 2017, she released her 21st album, *Medicine Songs*. Buffy continues to sing and protest with the same energy and outrage that have guided her career.

> 66
>
> *I really want this collection of songs to be like medicine, to be of some help or encouragement, to maybe do some good.*
>
> **—Buffy Sainte-Marie website:** *Medicine Songs*, 2017
>
> 99

In 1983, Buffy co-wrote a song for the movie An Officer and a Gentleman. *The song, "Up Where We Belong," won an Academy Award.*

Creating Art Beyond Music

Art and education have played important roles in Buffy's life and work. During her break from recording music, she completed a PhD degree in Fine Arts. She began to create large digital paintings of Indigenous and **mythological** figures. The collection was called *16 Million Colors*. Its images were daring and imaginative. It showcased Buffy's continued development as an artist and provided a new way for her to shine a spotlight on her Indigenous roots. It has been shown across North America.

Buffy has also created wearable art with her Elder Brothers digital image imprinted on the fabric.

Following Her Heart

Buffy's music has grown and matured from its early roots in folk music to include elements of rock, Indigenous rhythms, and techno beats. She has been labeled many things: a folk singer, a protest singer, a warrior for peace, and a social activist. But Buffy has really just followed her heart. She sings, makes art, and writes about what she believes in. She has been an inspiration to many—especially Indigenous artists. With a career spanning 50-plus years, Buffy's message and music continue to have an important place in today's world.

" *I just like people, love music, and seeing the world.*

—**Dazed Digital interview, 2012** **"**

In 2010, Canada honored Buffy with a Governor General's Performing Arts Award. It was presented by Governor General Michaëlle Jean.

? **THINK ABOUT IT**

How has Buffy's music developed over the years?

The Allan Waters Humanitarian Award Buffy received in 2017 is one of many she has earned during her life.

Awards and Recognition

Buffy has been recognized with numerous awards for her music and her activism

1993 – Established a new Juno Awards category for Aboriginal (Indigenous) music

1995 – Inducted into the Juno Hall of Fame

1997 – Native American Philanthropist of the Year

1997 – Officer of the Order of Canada (the highest honor granted to a Canadian)

2010 – Governor General's Performing Arts Award

2017 – Juno, Allan Walters Humanitarian Award

Writing Prompts

1. What role did Buffy's Indigenous heritage play in her life and music?

2. What are some of Buffy Sainte-Marie's most significant accomplishments?

3. How has Buffy used music, art, and film to support Indigenous issues?

4. What are some of her goals for Indigenous youth and communities in today's society?

5. What are some of the messages Buffy uses her music to deliver?

Learning More

Books

Long Powwow Nights by David Bouchard, Pam Aleekuk, and Buffy Sainte-Marie. Harper Red Deer Press, 2009.

Canadian Aboriginal Art and Culture: Cree by Erinn Banting. Weigl Educational Publishers, 2016.

The Salmon Twins by Caroll Simpson. Heritage House Publishing Company Ltd, 2013.

Stolen Words by Melanie Florence. Second Story Press, 2017.

The Honour Drum by Cheryl Bear and Tim Huff. Castle Quay Books, 2016.

The Kids Book of Aboriginal Peoples in Canada by Diane Silvey. Kids Can Press, 2012.

Websites

http://buffysainte-marie.com/
Official website of Buffy Sainte-Marie with information about her music, art, and philanthropy.

www.thecanadianencyclopedia.ca/en/article/cree/
History, culture, and traditional life of the Cree First Nation peoples.

www.nihewan.org
Nihewan Foundation for Native American Education website, the organization founded by Buffy Sainte-Marie to help promote education of and about Native American People and cultures.

www.thecanadianencyclopedia.ca/en/article/first-peoples-music/
Learn more about Aboriginal music and musicians – from Buffy Sainte-Marie to Tanya Tagaq and A Tribe Called Red.

Glossary

activism The support of strong actions or protests to help make changes in society

blacklisted Said that a person should be avoided

empower To give someone the power to seek changes or solutions

folk Traditional music that is passed through generations by oral tradition

humanity The qualities that make us human

Indigenous Describing plants, animals, or people who are native to an area

humanitarian A person who works to make other people's lives better

Mi'kmaq An Indigenous people from eastern Canada

mythological Something that is believed to be real by many people, but is not true

oppression Cruel and unjust treatment

philanthropy The practice of giving money or time to help make life better for other people

powwow A social gathering of Indigenous people that usually includes dancing

reserve A confined area of land where Indigenous people live

residential schools Boarding schools for Indigenous children that were enforced by the Canadian government

spirituality A person's search for a deeper meaning in life

stereotypes Unfair beliefs about all people who share a particular characteristic

synthesizer An electronic machine that produces and controls sounds for making music

Index